World's Greatest
SCIENTISTS
&
INVENTORS

Wonder House

(An imprint of Prakash Books)

Wonder
House
(An imprint of Prakash Books)

contact@wonderhousebooks.com

ISBN : 9789388369060

Contents

ALBERT EINSTEIN

BIRTH: March 14, 1879
Ulm, Germany

DEATH: April 18, 1955 (aged 76)
Princeton, New Jersey, USA

Albert Einstein was a German-born physicist famously known as the 'Father of Modern Physics'. He won the Nobel Prize in 1921. His major scientific work was the general theory of relativity. He is recognized as one of the most important physicists and mathematicians of the 21st century.

Albert Einstein was born on March 14, 1879, in Ulm, Germany to Hermann and Pauline Einstein. He had one younger sibling. His father worked in an electronics company. His love for science and physics developed because of his father. In 1880, his family moved to Munich, Germany. At the age of five, Einstein started his schooling at the Catholic Elementary School. His father gave the young Einstein a compass. The first thing he questioned was why the needle always pointed north on the compass.

He had an unbelievable brain capacity and was often called a genius. He also learned the violin from the age of six to thirteen. However, as a child, he had difficulty with his speech and was unable to speak fluently. But later in life, he did exceptionally well. He loved music all his life, as his mother was also a piano player.

In 1888, he went to the Luitpold Gymnasium. Einstein loved studying maths and science in school, especially calculus. In 1895, he attended a school in Aargau. The next year, he started to study at the Zurich Polytechnic in a teachers' training program. He was only seventeen years old when he was studying for his four-year mathematics and physics diploma program.

In 1900, he got the Zurich Polytechnic teaching diploma. Einstein continued his studies and received his doctoral degree in 1905. To complete his doctoral degree, he submitted research from which four of his papers got published in a prestigious physics journal of the time. That year, people began to see the birth of Einstein as an innovator and a great scientist.

He began working as a clerk at the Swiss patent office. During his job in the patent office, he published some of his major works in the field of science. In his free time, he would do scientific research. The major achievement of his life was researching about the theory of relativity and quantum theory in 1905. He changed the world and the history of science with his theories, which became the base for modern physics.

He made people think about the concepts of time, space and matter. Einstein was able to prove the impact of the solar eclipse with his theory of relativity. He created a new theory about the concept of gravity for he believed that the existing knowledge was inaccurate. Later he tested out his theories to be proven right.

Einstein shared his research on the nature of light, and how it is created because of small particles called photons. He was awarded the Nobel Prize for Physics in 1921 for this discovery. Einstein's brilliant theory of relativity helped in the invention of the atomic bomb. In 1911, he got a job at the Charles-Ferdinand University as a professor. Einstein worked as a professor most of his life. He was even a professor at Humboldt University. In 1916, after having had many academic successes, he was selected as the president of the German Physical Society. In 1921, Einstein's work was acknowledged by the Mayor of New York. He invited Einstein to stay in New York.

Soon, World War II broke out, which only ended in the year 1945. Einstein's theories were applied to create the atomic bomb by America during this war. By 1954, Einstein had written more than 300 scientific works. His theories are still used to study the universe and its laws. Many current experiments are based on Einstein's theories.

He was honored multiple times for his outstanding contribution to modern physics. In 1929, he was given the Max Planck Medal by the German Physical Society. He received the Franklin Institute's Franklin Medal for his discovery of relativity and photons.

Einstein and Mileva Maric married in the January of 1903. They were parents to three lovely children. But the marriage didn't last long and the couple got divorced in 1919. Einstein got married for the second time to a lady named Elsa in the same year. Elsa died in 1936, at the age of 76, after suffering from heart and kidney problems.

Einstein also had internal bleeding for which he refused to get surgery. He died on April 18, 1955. The same year, an element called 'Einsteinium' was included in the periodic table. In 1999, Einstein was named as the 'Person of the Century' by *Time* magazine. USA issued Einstein stamps as a tribute to the brilliant scientist.

ALEXANDER FLEMING

BIRTH: August 6, 1881
Ayrshire, Scotland

DEATH: March 11, 1955 (aged 73)
London, England

Sir Alexander Fleming was a great Scottish physicist, biologist and pharmacologist, who is known for his discovery of penicillin. It was the world's first antibiotic, which was used to treat bacterial infections and diseases. He also identified the enzyme 'lysozyme' in 1921. Fleming was the recipient of the Nobel Prize in Medicine in 1945.

Alexander Fleming was born on August 6, 1881 in Scotland to Hugh Fleming and Grace Stirling Morton.

He had seven siblings. He was born into a family of farmers. When he was only seven years old, he lost his father to ill health. To support his family, he started to work with his mother on the farm.

Fleming studied at Loudoun Moor School and Darvel School, and moved to London at the age of thirteen to attend the Royal Polytechnic Institution, after receiving scholarships for Kilmarnock Academy. He received an excellent education with the help of his mother. He took a few classes at Regent Street Polytechnic. After finishing his primary education, he followed his elder brother to the St Mary's Hospital Medical School on a scholarship. In 1908, he received a gold medal for being the top medical student there.

Fleming was offered a job in the research department at St Mary's as an assistant bacte-riologist. He wanted to become a surgeon, but started to take an interest in the field of bacteriology. During this time, he met Sir Almroth Edward Wright, who taught Fleming more about vaccines. His mentor, Wright guided Fleming to find medication to build the immune system, from what was available at the time.

At the time of World War I, Fleming served as a captain in the Royal Army Medical Corps. He worked in the war hospitals and kept researching the effects of antiseptics on the injuries. From his work, he found out that the antiseptic was doing more harm than good, and was also decreasing the patients' immunity which didn't allow them to heal properly. He mentioned that more soldiers were dying from the antiseptic treatment than from the infections they had picked up from injuries in the war. He suggested the solution that to heal the wounds they needed to be kept dry and clean. But, his observations were ignored.

While doing some tests in the laboratory, he discovered an enzyme called a 'lysozyme', which is usually present in tears, skin, hair and nails. Fleming was the first person to find this enzyme, which turned out to be one of the most important discoveries in the history of mankind. In today's medical field, lysozymes are used for treating colds and throat infections, and also as preservatives in food.

His next significant discovery was penicillin. Fleming made this discovery entirely by accident.

In 1928, Fleming was studying influenza when he stumbled upon the discovery. He was working on some germs which he was growing in his laboratory. After returning from a vacation, he noticed that a mold had started to grow on the plate. The germs were killed by the same mold. At first, he named it 'mold juice'; it was later renamed to 'penicillin'. It was a breakthrough in the field of science which could cure many diseases. In 1929, Fleming's findings were published in the *British Journal of Experimental Pathology*.

Even though Fleming found the mold, he couldn't find a way for its mass production. Until 1940, scientists Howard Florey and Ernst Boris Chain at Oxford continued with Fleming's research. They successfully turned the mold into medicine. The medicine started getting used in hospitals during World War II. Many battlefield infections were treated that earlier would have spread.

Fleming's development of penicillin continues to save millions of people around the world. The most significant accolade in his scientific career was winning the Nobel Prize in Medicine with two other scientists in 1945. He became an honorary member of every medical and scientific society of the time. He became the president of the Society for General Microbiology. He was awarded the Hunterian Professorship by the Royal College of Surgeons of England. Fleming was knighted by King George VI and became Sir Alexander Fleming in 1944.

Fleming married Sarah Marion, a nurse, on December 24, 1915. The couple had one son, who also studied medicine. Fleming died at the age of 73 due to a heart attack on March 11, 1955.

ALEXANDER GRAHAM BELL

BIRTH: March 3, 1847
Edinburgh, Scotland

DEATH : August 2, 1922 (aged 75)
Beinn Bhreagh, Canada

Alexander Graham Bell was a Scottish-American inventor, scientist, businessman and a great teacher. He was the inventor of the telephone, by which he created history in the field of communication. He was described as the 'teacher of the deaf', and started the well-known Bell Telephone Company.

Alexander Graham Bell was born on March 3, 1847

in Edinburgh, Scotland to Prof. Alexander Melville Bell and Eliza Grace Symonds. He had two siblings. He got the name 'Graham' at the age of ten. Alexander wanted to have a middle name, like his two brothers, and so he became Alexander Graham Bell.

He was born into a well-educated family. The young Alexander was taught by his grandfather, who was a speech teacher. His father was a teacher and taught deaf children how to speak. His mother was deaf, and a talented painter. She also played the piano. Alexander was home-schooled by his mother and later went to Edinburgh's Royal High School. After graduating, he attended the University of Edinburgh and the University College London. In 1864, Alexander got the position of a pupil-teacher at Weston House Academy, Moray.

His first invention was creating a wheat-husking machine at the age of twelve. In 1870, his family settled in Canada after the death of his two brothers. Two years later, Alexander started the School of Vocal Physiology and Mechanics of Speech in Boston. He helped his students learn the manner of speech. Greatly influenced by his family, he started to work with deaf people. With his father, he developed 'Visible Speech'. It was the study of how the tongue, lips and throat are used to produce vocal sounds.

In 1872, he became a professor at the Boston University School of Oratory. Along with his teaching job, Bell continued to work on his own research. He focused his research on his father's work of teaching deaf people to interact. This was the start of Bell's journey towards the invention of the telephone. He worked on the idea of transmitting human voice over wires, and began working on how to transmit telephonic messages. He conducted experiments and attempted to send multiple telegraph signals over a single cable.

The first time he speculated inventing the telephone was in 1874. He finally came up with a discovery to successfully send multiple messages on a single wire. Bell listened to the human voice over a wire which led to the invention the of telephone. He finally got the patent in 1876, which is considered as one of the most valuable patents in history. The first words that were spoken on the phone in his laboratory were, "Mr Watson—come here—I want to see you." In 1877, Bell started the Bell Telephone Company.

Apart from this, he invented many other things in the field of science. Bell made the first metal detector in the world. He also developed the audiometer, which was used to detect hearing problems. He even created a device to help find icebergs. In 1888, Bell was one of the founding members of the National Geographic. It later became one of the most famous magazines in the world.

Bell worked for the deaf all his life. He developed many new techniques and helped teach lip-reading teaching. In 1890, he started the Alexander Graham Bell Association for the Deaf. At the end of the nineteenth century, he began to take an interest in transport technologies instead of sound and recording. In 1907, he founded the Aerial Experiment Association and conducted outstanding work in the field of hydrofoils and aeronautics. He also created high speed aircrafts and boats. Bell, with a few others, made many flying machines; the most famous one was the Silver Dart. It was the first machine that was flown in Canada.

Bell created history with his inventions, which changed the world. He was honored for these several times in his career. He was awarded the Volta Prize along with a cash prize in 1880 for the invention of the telephone. In 1881, the Government of France honored him with the Legion of Honor and then the Albert Medal in 1902. In 1914, he received AIEE's Edison Medal for honorable achievement for the invention of the telephone. He also received many honorary degrees from academic institutions.

Bell married Mabel Hubbard in 1877. She was one of Alexander's deaf students and ten years younger to him. The couple had four children. He passed away on August 2, 1922. On his burial day, as a tribute, all the telephone services in the United States were halted for a minute.

BENJAMIN FRANKLIN

BIRTH: January 17, 1706
Boston, Massachusetts, USA

DEATH: April 17, 1790 (aged 84)
Philadelphia, Pennsylvania, USA

Benjamin Franklin was an American scientist, philosopher, innovator and writer. He was one of the Founding Fathers of the United States. He was called the 'First American'. He invented various things throughout his life like swim fins, catheters, library chairs, step ladders, lightning rods, bifocal glasses and the Franklin stove. He contributed to science majorly through the field of electricity. He also helped form the Constitution of the United States.

Benjamin Franklin was born on January 17, 1706, in Massachusetts to Josiah Franklin and Abiah Folger. His father owned a candle-making business and his brother had a printing shop. He grew up in a large family and had sixteen siblings. Benjamin worked in his father's candle and soap shop. But he wasn't interested in this work. Due to his family's financial conditions, Benjamin had to discontinue his education. He left school at the age of ten. He always loved reading and mastered many skills just by reading books. Even though he attended school for only two years, he learned foreign languages, grammar, science and maths. At the age of twelve, he started to work in his brother's printing shop and learned the basics of business.

He was a great writer and wrote many articles. One of his works was published in the *New England Courant*. However, his father and brother didn't support his writing. When Benjamin was only seventeen, he left the family business and traveled to Philadelphia. He got a job in a printing shop. He then went to London and got a typesetter's job. In 1725, he wrote his first pamphlet, *A Dissertation upon Liberty and Necessity, Pleasure and Pain.*

At the age of 21, he started a Junto Club where people with similar tastes or opinions would meet. The group started the first library in America, when there were very limited books available to read. They collected books on various genres and displayed them in the library.

Franklin bought a newspaper called the *Pennsylvania Gazette* in 1733. He also wrote cooking recipes, predictions and weather reports in his *Poor Richard's Almanack.* He helped the society in many ways. In 1736, he founded the first volunteer firefighting company called the Union Fire Company. In 1743, Franklin founded the American Philosophical Society. Many organizations that were started by him still exist today. He also worked as a postmaster and formed a practical postal system.

During 1748, Franklin was considered as one of the richest men in Pennsylvania. He was one of the Founding Fathers of the United States. He worked as an ambassador for England. He warned the British government about the risks of taxes. His major contribution was writing the Declaration of Independence and the Constitution of the United States. Franklin was also against slavery. He was the first person to raise his voice about this issue.

Franklin's most intriguing discovery was noticing electricity in lightning. He performed many tests and proved that lightning is in fact constituted of electricity.

He invented bifocal glasses for people with weak eyesight in 1784. Franklin's most famous discovery was the Gulf Stream. When he traveled across the Atlantic Ocean in 1775, he accidentally unearthed the Gulf Stream.

Some of his major works include *The Autobiography of Benjamin Franklin* written from 1771-90. In 1758, he published *The Way to Wealth*. These two books became his bestsellers. He even wrote a guidebook which helped handle finances. He also taught entrepreneurial skills to readers, which he had learned in his early years.

In 1753, he received the Royal Society's Copley Medal for his invention in the field of electricity. The same year, he was honored with degrees from Harvard as well as Yale University for his scientific work.

Franklin got married to Deborah Reed in 1730. They had three children.

He died on April 17, 1790, at the age of 84 in Pennsylvania. Thousands of people attended Franklin's funeral. He fought to change people's lives and left a great legacy behind. He touched many lives because of his love for humanity. After his death, the Benjamin Franklin Award was introduced. His images were also used in dollar bills and stamps. He was known as the 'First American' and many areas in America such as the North Franklin Township, Nebraska and North Franklin are named after Benjamin Franklin.

DMITRI MENDELEEV

BIRTH : *February 8, 1834*
Tobolsk, Russia

DEATH : *February 2, 1907 (aged 72)*
St Petersburg, Russia

Dmitri Mendeleev was a Russian chemist who formulated the periodic law. He classified the elements in the periodic table. He also foretold the properties of three of the possible elements.

Dmitri Mendeleev was born on February 8, 1834, in Russia, to Ivan Pavlovich Mendeleev and Maria Dmitrievna Mendeleev. Dmitri had a tough childhood after the death of his father. For a short while, Dmitri's family survived on his father's pension. But it was not enough, so they started to work in a glass factory. Another disaster struck Dmitri's family. The glass factory, which his mother used to run, was burned down. The family moved on to settle in St Petersburg.

Dmitri graduated from the Main Pedagogical Institute in 1855 and got a master's degree in chemistry in 1856. During hard times, he still pursued his dream and worked hard. He learned mathematics, physics and chemistry.

After studying overseas for some time, Dmitri went back to St Petersburg and worked as a professor. After he completed his studies in chemistry, he realized that there were few good chemistry textbooks available. To resolve this issue, Dmitri researched and worked on his own books. He went to an international conference in which scientists who were interested in atoms and elements had gathered. This impacted the young Dmitri, who started to think about the different elements in chemistry. He soon wrote his thesis, *On the Combinations of Water with Alcohol.*

Mendeleev even came up with a complete textbook of organic chemistry. It was a 500-page textbook. He won the Demidov Prize for the success of this book. He became a member of many popular scientific societies. His lectures were attended by a large number of students from various departments.

His major contribution to science was discovering the periodic table of elements for which he used the periodic law. In 1869, his research caught the attention of the famous Russian Chemical Society, and the society's newspaper published his work and findings about the atomic weights of the elements. In 1870, Mendeleev explained the periodic law. He released his second book *The Principles of Chemistry* in two volumes in 1868 and 1870, respectively. The book became very popular and was translated into French, German and English.

Not only did he discover the periodic table, but he also predicted three of the possible elements which needed to be found. While he worked on the table, he left an empty space for a new chemical element whose but he also predicted three of the possible elements which needed to be found. While he worked on the table, he left an empty space for a new chemical element whose properties were entirely different from the other elements in its group. When those three elements were eventually discovered, Mendeleev's periodic table of elements was proven accurate.

Mendeleev's periodic table of elements set the foundation for the development of modern chemistry. The table itself is flexible and is still developing. At the end of the nineteenth century, Mendeleev retired from his university position. He got involved in government-related work.

He propounded various theories on mass, weight and gases. He also proposed that there are many important chemical compounds present in petroleum. He was not only good at chemistry, but he also took an interest in solar eclipses, the movement of the pendulum clock, mining, and polar ice. Mendeleev mastered physics, natural sciences, and economics. He was awarded the Copley Medal in 1905. He received the highest honor for his discovery of the periodic table by after twenty years of marriage, the couple got divorced. In 1882, he married Anna Ivanova Popova. He was the father of six children.

Mendeleev died on February 2, 1907, at the age of 72 in St Petersburg, Russia. As a tribute on his funeral day, many people bought copies of the periodic table. A crater on the moon, a planetoid, and element number 101 were named after him.

ELI WHITNEY

BIRTH: *December 8, 1765*
Westborough, Massachusetts, USA

DEATH: *January 8, 1825 (aged 59)*
New Haven, Connecticut, USA

Eli Whitney was an American inventor, engineer and manufacturer, famously known for his invention of the cotton gin. He created a machine which was used in removing seeds from cotton fiber. It was one of the key inventions of the Industrial Revolution.

Eli Whitney was born on December 8, 1765, in Massachusetts to Eli Whitney, Sr. and Elizabeth. His father was a farmer who had an interest in mechanical work. Because of his father, Eli turned towards machinery and technology at an early age. Eli started to work while pursuing his studies to support his family. He used to build different devices. He helped his father on the farm and also worked as a school teacher to earn more money.

After completing his high school education, he attended Yale College. In 1792, he graduated from college. Eli wanted to become a lawyer. However, he struggled financially and had to tutor in South Carolina. Fortunately, he got an invitation to stay with Catherine Greene in 1755. The lady wanted Eli to visit her plantation Mulberry Grove, in Georgia. It was the first time that Eli learned about cotton production. He realized that cotton farmers faced many difficulties in making a living.

At the time, farming the cotton crop was the primary source of income for people. It was easy to grow and could be stored for a long period of time. The main problem was separating the cotton seeds from the soft fiber. It took a lot of time and labor for this kind of work. The average person could remove the seeds from only about one pound of cotton per day, which was a very small amount. Greene shared the problem of the short staple cotton with Whitney.

Catherine Greene helped Whitney to build a machine that was able to quickly and efficiently clean the cotton plants, and a machine called the 'cotton gin', in which the word 'gin' stood for the word 'engine'. His machine could clean up to 55 pounds of cotton daily. This helped massively in America's economic development. The machine worked like a filter in which cotton was run through a wooden drum installed with a series of hooks that caught the fibers. Then the fibers were removed through a net, leaving the clean cotton behind.

Whitney presented his cotton gin to the common people. They were amazed to see that the machine could clean a large amount of cotton in less than an hour. People liked his device and wanted to utilize it for their own businesses. Whitney finally patented his invention in 1794. In just a few months, he started a cotton gin manufacturing company. He planned to install the cotton gins throughout the country and charge farmers a small amount for each plantation. The farmers welcomed the invention, but they refused to share a percentage of their profits with Whitney. As a result, the farmers made their own cotton gins and Whitney's invention was pirated. Many of them were an improved version of Whitney's original model. He sadly couldn't protect his invention from being pirated. The patent law at the time lacked in protecting the inventor's rights. But, as more people started to use the cotton gin by the mid-nineteenth century, cotton became America's leading trade.

The piracy debacle did not deter Whitney and he continued to invent many more devices and machines. In 1798, he signed a contract with the US government to produce arms and weapons. He was asked to make 10,000 pieces of military equipment in two years to help the government in the war against France. But it eventually took Whitney around ten years to actually develop those many devices. After fulfilling the government's demand, he soon received another order for 15,000 pieces of military equipment, which he managed to supply in two years. Whitney's great contribution has led him to being called the 'Father of American Technology'. He was recognized for inventing the first milling machine.

Whitney got married to Henrietta Edwards in 1817. The couple had four children. His wife belonged to high society, and it helped Whitney to progress to an elite class. Whitney died at the age of 59 in 1825 due to cancer, in New Haven.

GEORGE STEPHENSON

BIRTH: June 9, 1781
Wylam, England

DEATH: August 12, 1848 (aged 67)
Chesterfield, England

George Stephenson was an English engineer and the inventor of the railway line, which eventually became the global standard size for all rail tracks and was even called the 'Stephenson gauge'. He also created the miners' safety lamp.

George Stephenson was born on June 9, 1781, in Wylam, England to Robert and Mabel Stephenson. He was the couple's second child. His father was a fireman and worked in a coal mine. His family was poor and George could not afford to go to school. So, he worked and helped his family earn money. During the nights, he taught himself how to read and write. He then took an interest in mathematics.

He worked on a farm and by the time he was ten, he had learned horse riding. At the age of seventeen, he took a job in a coal mine as an engineer. In his next job, he worked as a brakeman. To earn extra money, he took up additional work like repairing shoes and clocks. In 1811, he got a raise at High Pit, Killingworth Colliery, when he fixed a broken pumping engine. He became an expert in steam-driving engineering. He studied machines and engines to develop a better understanding of steam machines. He was always busy conducting different experiments.

Stephenson's most significant invention took place at the age of 33. He made his first locomotive in 1814. He used the steam engine which led to its success. The machine was called 'Blucher' and was created to carry coal. It was the first steam engine train that ran on the railroad. It was designed to pull tons of coal up hills and had eight wagons. Stephenson's rail became the most successful steam engine ever built. The first few Blucher rides broke down, but each failure made him improve the design. Each time, he came up with a more powerful engine, and it doubled the amount of coal that could be carried.

He spent most of his life in the coal mines. He thought of an invention which could minimize the risk of explosion. The Royal Society also announced a large reward for the invention of a successful lamp. Stephenson created the safety lamp in 1815. The cylinder lamp had tiny air holes that reduced exposure.

His locomotive steam engine became famous amongst the locals and he soon made more locomotives for Killingworth. In 1820, he built the first railways, which were completely steam-powered. He got a patent for his cast iron rails. He was selected as an engineer to create the Stockton and Darlington railways. In 1825, the first public railways were opened. The first locomotive was named 'Locomotion'. It was the first engine to have a passenger car. The same year, his gauge, used in the construction of tracks, became the world's standard gauge. It was called the 'Stephenson gauge'.

Stephenson's Stockton and Darlington rail-way projects were also successful. Before this, the trains were only used to carry coal. The Stephenson railways opened up business for other trades. It became easier to transport cloth or fabrics produced in Manchester to Liverpool. The project was very profitable.

In 1829, Stephenson entered a competition to design a train. Stephenson designed his train called 'Rocket', which won the prize. Soon, his train and railway techniques were adopted by United States too. In 1830, the Liverpool and Manchester Railway was opened to the public. People came from different places to see this new technology. The Prime Minister, the Duke of Wellington was amongst them.

Stephenson is one of the few inventors who are greatly remembered for their immense contributions to society that brought about revolutionary changes.

The impact of the railroad spread quickly throughout Britain, Europe and North America. Stephenson was offered many projects and continued to build railways for the rest of his life. While he made railways and tracks, he also had to construct tunnels and holes. In the process, he discovered new coal fields which made him even wealthier. He made journeys shorter and contributed to the new industrial age.

Stephenson was married three times and had two children. He was named as 'the Father of the Railways'. He died on 12th August, 1848, in Derbyshire at the age of 67.

GUGLIELMO MARCONI

BIRTH: *April 25, 1874*
Bologna, Italy

DEATH: *July 20, 1937 (aged 63)*
Rome, Italy

Guglielmo Marconi was an Italian engineer, physicist and inventor. Marconi successfully invented the long-distance wireless telegraph and the radio signal. He majorly contributed to the development of the radio and won the Nobel Prize in Physics in 1909.

Guglielmo Marconi was born in 1874 in Bologna, Italy to Giuseppe Marconi and Anne Jameson. Both his parents were working. His family had to travel a lot due to their silk business. During these trips, Marconi was tutored by different people. For the first few years, he was educated privately in Bologna.

He studied languages. Marconi started to read various books on science and electricity. He completed his education at the Livorno Technical Institute and then went to the University of Bologna. He developed an interest in the field of electricity at a very young age. He performed many experiments in a small room in his house. After he completed his education, he entirely focused on his electricity-related projects. His family was very supportive of his interests, especially his mother.

Marconi's work was heavily influenced by Heinrich Hertz. He was amazed by Hertz's discovery of invisible waves, created by electro-magnetic interactions called 'Hertzian waves'. Marconi was only fourteen when he first heard of Hertz's work.

In 1895, he developed a communication model which made wireless radio signaling possible. So, he set up a laboratory in his father's home for his experiments. His university professor helped Marconi with his experiments. At the age of 21, he performed his first successful experiment. He sent different signals over a distance of more than one mile.

At the age of 22, Marconi traveled to England with his mother. He found some interested sponsors for his experiments. One of them was the British Post Office. London was the commercial and financial hub of England. He wanted to show his experiments to the public who could buy them. Marconi met Preece, who was impressed by his experiments and decided to help him financially.

Marconi performed the first experiment on the rooftops of two buildings in London, which was a success. In 1896, Marconi got the patent for wireless telegraphy. The same year, he decided to open his own company. With the help of his family, he started Wireless Telegraphy & Signal Company Limited. Marconi built the first radio station of the world in 1897. And the next year, he created the world's first wireless telegraph factory in England.

At the end of the eighteenth century, Marconi sent signals across the English Channel and established wireless communication between France and England. In 1901, he sent the most powerful radio signal broadcast. He made an antenna attached to a balloon. He was the first person to pick up the faint three-dot sequence of the Morse code letter 's'. In 1908, Marconi set up a service to send telegrams between the UK and Canada. It was the first commercial use of wireless services.

In 1909, he was awarded the Nobel Prize in Physics, which he shared with Ferdinand Braun. Marconi had many of his inventions patented; one being the 'magnetic detector'. It was used as a standard wireless receiver for many years.

In the beginning, most of Marconi's inven-tions were rejected by the Italian government. The Italian government later realized how they had failed to respect such a great scientist.

Marconi also served in the Italian navy and army as a lieutenant. During World War I, he helped the military with his wireless services. He started developing the shortwave radio technology. He called it the 'Marconi Radio' and installed it on ships.

For his significant contribution to science and technology, he was not only awarded the Nobel Prize in Physics but was also honored with the Albert Medal, the Kelvin Medal and the John Fritz Medal.

Marconi married twice and was the father of five children. He died on July 20, 1937, at the aged of 63, after he suffered from multiple heart attacks. As a tribute, radio stations in America, England and Italy broadcasted a few minutes of silence for the great inventor.

JAMES WATT

BIRTH: January 19, 1736
Greenock, Scotland

DEATH: August 25, 1819 (aged 83)
Birmingham, England

James Watt was a Scottish inventor, mechanical engineer, and chemist. He is known for his invention of the first modern steam engine. He played a significant role in the Industrial Revolution by developing mathematical instruments and later, steam engines. He was a renowned member of the Royal Society of London.

James Watt was born on 19th January, 1736 in Greenock, Scotland to Agnes Muirhead and James Watt. He came from a well-educated family. His father was a businessman and a contractor. He was often home-schooled by his mother in the subjects of arithmetic and writing. His love for machinery started when his father gifted him a small toolkit. He played with it at his father's workshop. He also deconstructed and reassembled different objects. As a kid, he designed various models and instruments.

While growing up he faced some difficult times due to his family's financial condition. His father lost his inheritance. At the age of seventeen, James lost his mother; he was devastated. At this time, one of his relatives working at Glasgow University inspired James to master the skill of instrument-making. He went to London and used his skills to earn money. He decided to pursue a career in mathematical-instrument making. He learned how to craft the instruments from his father and grandfather.

In 1755, Watt started working in an instrument-making workshop. There, he met John Morgan who taught him the craft of making instruments with a little pay. In just one year, Watt learned all the necessary skills and made a successful career out of it. Even though

Watt never had any musical talent, his instruments were better than those made by music experts. Next year, he returned to Glasgow to start his own business of instrument-making. In 1757, Watt set up his shop at the university campus with his friend. For the next six years, Watt and John Craig built many musical instruments and toys. He was known as the 'mathematical instrument maker' at the university. During this time, he met the famous economist Adam Smith.

Watt developed an interest in building the steam engine. He met John Robinson, who introduced Watt to the science and technology behind it. He first got the chance to make an instrument, when one of his professors directed his attention towards a Newcomen steam en-gine that was not working properly. Thomas Newcomen had built the engine to pump out the water in the mines. James knew that he could use this engine for more than just pumping water. He saw the potential and the profit in it.

For many years, he worked on this model. It took him a lot of time to design it. In 1775, he came up with a method to change and improve the engine, which led to the invention of the modern steam engine. He was the first person to suggest a separate condenser for the engine.

In 1775, he got a patent for his steam engine called 'A New Invented Method of Lessening the Consumption of Steam and Fuel in Fire Engines'. The invention of the steam engine played a major role in the Industrial Revolution and helped Great Britain with its economic growth.

Watt replicated the previous Newcomen model to improve the production method. Watt opened the Boulton & Watt Company with Matthew Boulton, where they sold steam engines. The demand for his engine grew all over the world. Watt's company employed many people to run the business, which benefited the society. In 1784, Watt made further improvements to the steam engine and patented his steam locomotive. By the end of the seventeenth century, both Watt and Boulton were wealthy men. He retired a few years later and used his wealth to pursue other interests like improving oil lamps and measuring distances with a telescope.

For his significant contribution to the society, he received many awards. In 1784, Watt became a member of the Royal Society of Edinburgh. In 1787, he was selected as a member of the Batavian Society for Experimental Philosophy. In 1806, he was awarded an honorary doctorate in law by the University of Glasgow. After his death, James' last name 'Watt' was included in the unit of power in the International System of Units.

Watt married Margaret Miller in 1764. She died while giving birth. He got married for the second time in 1777 to Ann Macgregor.

James died at the age of 83, on 25th August, 1819 in England.

JOHANNES GUTENBERG

BIRTH: ca. 1399
Mainz, Germany

DEATH: February 2, 1468
Mainz, Germany

Johannes Gutenberg was a German goldsmith, printer, publisher and also a well-known inventor. He was the first person to introduce the movable-type printing press in Europe, which was used until the twentieth century. He introduced the first-ever printed book with the movable type called *Forty-Two-Line Bible* or the *Gutenberg Bible*.

Johannes Gutenberg was born around 1399 in Mainz, Germany, to Friele Gensfleisch zur Laden and

Else Wyrich. He was the youngest in his family. His father was a well-known merchant.

From a very young age, Johannes took an interest in reading. The books that he used to read were written by hand. These were known as 'manuscripts', which implied 'hand written'. He belonged to a wealthy family, to whom books were easily available. Johannes wanted other people to be able to afford these books as well, so he decided to create a quicker way of printing. The earliest widely used printing machine and method was known as 'block printing'. The machine was made of wooden blocks, and each block would print only one page at a time. It was the slowest method of producing copies of books.

In 1428, Gutenberg got a job in the jewelry industry. He learned how to cut gems and make jewelry. Gutenberg did most of his experiments in secret. He turned his home into a workshop, where he worked day and night. He often felt disappointed as most of his experiments failed. He suffered financial crises, as he invested most of his savings in his experiments.

He met Johann Fust, a wealthy goldsmith and lawyer at his old home, Mainz in 1448. Fust helped Gutenberg financially and Gutenberg continued his work. In just two years, his new printing press machine was ready.

He came up with many ideas for creating this printing machine. First, Gutenberg designed a little hardwood block, which printed a single letter at a time. It was a very slow process. Then, he moved to movable types, which printed only one page. He believed that using wood for printing was the reason behind his failure. So, Gutenberg moved away from wood types and decided to use metal types. It was a success, and he was able to print his first book in a few years. His business grew and he got into a partnership with Johann Fust, who helped him with his business. But soon, Fust blamed Gutenberg for spending his money and not creating any profit in return. Gutenberg lost his business eventually and all the rights went to Fust.

The first pieces printed from the press were German poems. Soon, he started to print the Latin Bible and Latin grammar texts.

Gutenberg's most famous work was the 300-page book, the *Gutenberg Bible,* with each page containing 42 lines.

These books, for the first time, were available to people outside the church. He opened his second workshop at his birthplace, Mainz. Everyone in Europe knew about Gutenberg at this point and his feat of mass production of books. He printed hundreds of Bibles in very little time.

The Gutenberg press was a major invention in world history. The books evolved from handwritten to printed books. It all became possible due to Gutenberg's hard work and dedi-cation. He introduced the fast printing press, which decreased the cost of books and saved time. The Gutenberg press continued to be used in the nineteenth and twentieth centuries. The works printed by him are considered rare and constitute some of the most valuable printed material in the world.

He received the title of Hofmann for his

scientific work. He was called a 'Gentleman of the Court'. The honor came with money, clothing and food, which was provided to him until his death.

Gutenberg died in 1468 in Mainz, Germany and left a great legacy behind. His prints achieved great fame, and sold millions of copies all over the world. Project Gutenberg, the oldest digital library, was built as a tribute to Gutenberg. In 1952, the United States released stamps to honor Gutenberg's invention. *Time* magazine declared that the Gutenberg invention was the most crucial work in the history of inventions. A minor planet called '777 Gutenberga' was named after him. He is still remembered as a great printer and innovator.

JOSEPH PRIESTLEY

BIRTH: *March 13, 1733*
Birstall, England

DEATH: *February 6, 1804 (aged 70)*
Pennsylvania, USA

Joseph Priestley was an English priest, author, chemist and scientist, who made one of the most significant contributions to the field of experimental chemistry with his discovery of oxygen.

Joseph Priestley was born on 13th March, 1733 in England to Jonas Priestley and Mary Swift. He was the eldest of six children. He belonged to an English family and his parents were cloth makers. He received his early education at a grammar school. From a very young age, Priestley was interested in politics, religion and science. He studied Latin and Greek, and became skilled in physics, philosophy and mathematics. His father sent him to live with his uncle and aunt. After he completed his education at the local school, he went to Daventry Academy. Priestly completed his education and worked as a minister and a teacher.

During the 1760s, Priestly met many English intellectuals. In 1765, he was made a Doctor of Law by the University of Edinburgh for his *A Chart of Biography*. The next year, his experiments with electricity made him a member of the Royal Society. His involvement in religious and political philosophies led him to become friends with leaders like Benjamin Franklin, John Adams and Thomas Jefferson.

Benjamin Franklin was Priestley's good friend and supported his work in science and politics. Priestley's most significant research was the 700-page long *The*

History and Present State of Electricity. Priestley's other major work was *The Rudiments of English Grammar,* a famous grammar book written in 1761. He opened a local school where children were taught English grammar and other languages.

In 1765, he released *Essay on a Course of Liberal Education for Civil and Active Life.* In his essay, he discussed how universities don't allow their students to learn practical skills which could be of use in the real world. Instead, children were given a traditional and classical education. Later, he published a book called *A History of the Corruptions of Christianity.* This was the most significant of all his works as an author. Priestley soon became a well-established author and people liked reading his works. He became one of the most respected members of Britain's scientific community.

Priestley also established himself as a renowned chemist. One of his most significant discoveries was oxygen. He conducted many experiments to analyze the different properties of air. He tested oxygen separately to see if it would support life. Then one day, he made an important observation: plants released oxygen into the air. Between 1772 and 1790, he wrote six volumes of *Experiments and Observations on Different Kinds of Air*. He explained the ways by which he discovered oxygen. The word 'oxygen' was derived from the Greek word for 'acid-maker'.

PriestleywasknowntobeasupporteroftheAmerican Revolution. He also published many controversial works and supported the French Revolution. During 1791, his writings led to a massive negative response from the public and the government. His house and church were burned down, after which he fled the country with his family. He settled in Pennsylvania, United States and spent the latter years of his life there.

Priestley continued his research and made more significant contributions to chemistry. He experimented and separated carbon monoxide. It was termed as 'heavy inflammable air'. He also built the Unitarian Church in the United States. In 1876, the American Chemical Society was founded because of Priestley's discovery of oxygen. Currently, it is the world's largest scientific society.

Many statues of Priestley have been built all over Britain as a tribute to his inventions. Since 1922, the Priestley Medal has been awarded to those scientists who contributed towards the welfare of humanity.

Priestley got married on 23rd June, 1762 to Mary Wilkinson. The couple had four children. He died at the age of seventy on 6th February, 1804.

KARL BENZ

BIRTH: *November 25, 1844*
Karlsruhe, German

DEATH: *April 4, 1929 (aged 84)*
Ladenburg, Germany

Karl Friedrich Benz was a German engineer and entrepreneur, who designed and built the world's first automobile powered by an internal-combustion engine. Karl Benz was the founder of Mercedes-Benz.

Karl Benz's real name was Karl Friedrich Michael Vaillant. He was born on 25th November, 1844 in Germany to Josephine Vaillant and Johann Georg Benz. Karl's father worked as a locomotive driver. He lost his father at a very young age. His family was poor but Karl's mother provided him with the best education.

Karl went to a local grammar school. He was a great student and worked hard to get a good education. He followed his father's footsteps and took an interest in automobiles. Later, he attended the Polytechnical University, Karslruhe. In 1864, at the age of nineteen, he graduated in mechanical engineering.

After he graduated, Benz started a mechanical workshop with his friend. They sold building and construction material. However, the company came out as a total failure in just one year. Benz then began to work in a bicycle repair workshop. It was working with bicycles that made him think about a mechanized vehicle. His knowledge about the bicycle came in handy. He wanted to make carriages that did not need the help of horses for movement.

Benz was determined to make this dream come true. He developed a new and better engine for his carriers. During 1885, Benz designed many parts of his automobile. To earn more money for his family, Benz gave birth to many inventions and patented most of them. These include the ignition, spark plug, gearshift, water radiator, and clutch. He created a four-stroke engine for the carriage. The engine was placed between the rear wheels of the carriage. He designed his automobile in such a way that many people could sit in it. Benz was the first person to use the first fully-powered gas car with two seats, one each for a driver and a passenger. In 1885, he completed his breakthrough invention. It was the very first automobile that was ready for commercial use. In 1886, he got the patent for his engine.

Benz was ready to sell his great invention. His invention changed the lives of people who wished to travel long distances. However, in the beginning, it was hard for Benz to show its benefits. People were not convinced that it was much better than the horse carriages that they used at the time. People didn't buy Benz's idea and found it impractical, until his wife Bertha took the first long-distance tour in it. The goal was to build awareness in the automobile industry and change the public's opinion. She was successful in attempting this tour.

Benz's automobile was then considered to be the safest means of transportation.

Benz kept on improving his automobile model, as it gained popularity and demand amongst people. One flaw in his earlier model was that it couldn't be driven on high hills. Also, getting fuel for these automobiles was difficult. He added brake linings and an extra gear for the ability to drive over hills.

The World Fair held in Paris, in 1889 increased the demand for his cars. He then set up new infrastructure for building more automobiles. He first launched the 'Benz Model 1' in 1885 and then the 'Benz Model 2'. Soon, the 'Model 3' was also available. Benz came up with a major change in his next design and introduced the 'Benz Velo' model. It had four wheels instead of three.

Benz faced intense competition in 1920 from Daimler, who was the maker of the Mercedes engine. Both companies were in high demand. So, in 1924, they signed an agreement of mutual interest. It benefited both of them and saved them money due to their combined production, marketing, purchasing and advertising efforts. Soon, the two companies ventured as Daimler-Benz and created one of the most famous brands in the world: Mercedes-Benz. The decision was fruitful for both the companies. In 1927, they launched diesel trucks.

Benz and Bertha got married in 1872. They had five children. Bertha helped her husband start the business and establish the brand, which became well-known all over the world.

Benz died on April 4, 1929, at the age of 84, at his home in Germany. Benz left a great legacy after his death and made a significant contribution to the history of automobiles. He is a prime example of innovation and marketing that continues to be used in the automobile industry.

LEE DE FOREST

BIRTH: *August 26, 1873*
Council Bluffs, Iowa, USA

DEATH: *June 30, 1961 (aged 87)*
Hollywood, California, USA

Lee de Forest was an American inventor who invented the Audion vacuum tube, which was used in radios. He was known as the 'Father of Radio' and the 'Grandfather of Television'. Forest was also hailed as one of the founders of the electronic age.

Lee de Forest was born on August 26, 1873, in Iowa to Henry Swift de Forest and Anna Robbins. His father worked in the ministry and wanted his son to follow the same path. But, young Lee wanted to become an inventor and loved science. He used to take interest in machinery as a kid. For his education, Lee went to Mount Hermon School. After he graduated, he attended the Sheffield Scientific School at Yale in 1893. He continued his studies and achieved his dream of becoming an engineer. In 1899, he earned a PhD in physics and submitted his thesis titled *Reflection of Hertzian Waves from the Ends of Parallel Wires.* The renowned physicist Willard Gibbs helped him with his thesis.

After he graduated from Yale, he started looking for jobs. He began working at the Western Electric Company. Forest carried out experiments and created an electrolytic detector of Hertzian waves. In 1902, he opened his own company called the American De Forest Wireless Telegraph firm. He developed and sold radio equipment. He planned to earn money from his inventions, but his business partners deceived him. In just a few years his company went bankrupt.

In 1906, he created an electronic vacuum tube, the 'Audion'. It was known as the first electronic device that converted a weak sound into a stronger signal. He then developed a three-electrode device, which was used to detect the electromagnetic waves. In 1913, he sold the patent for this invention.

Forest established another company named The Radio Telephone Company. But his second company failed as well. In 1911, he was offered a research job at the Federal Telegraph Company. Forest's major work came about in 1916 when he broadcasted the first radio advertisement. He even aired the presidential election report on the radio.

The next five years, he fully concentrated on his new inventions. He stopped most of his radio research and developed an optical sound-on-film system, the Phonofilm. He called it the 'De Forest Phonofilm process'. In 1922, he started the De Forest Phonofilm Company. The Phonofilm was able to send sound directly onto the film. It was used to record stage performances, speeches and music concerts. Hollywood also began to use sound-on-film systems, and it was quite profitable.

Forest premiered eighteen short films, made in Phonofilm, on April 15, 1923, at the Rivoli Theater in New York City. In 1926, Hollywood introduced a new method for sound film. The sound-on-disc process was developed by the Warner Brothers. But Forest's Phonofilm was still in demand. Almost 200 short films were made by the Phonofilm process, and many are stored in the collections of the Library of Congress and the British Film Institute.

Forest was also linked to politics. He was a conservative Republican and an anti-communist. But, he eventually reduced his involvement in politics.

Forest was lauded for his significant contribution to science and technology. He received many awards and honors for his inventions. In 1922, he was given the IRE Medal of Honor for his contributions to radio. He was also awarded the Edison Medal by the American Institute of Electrical Engineers.

In 1957, Forest was a guest celebrity on the television

show *This Is Your Life*. He was introduced as the 'Father of Radio and the Grandfather of Television'. He even authored an autobiography named *Father of Radio*. He suffered a severe heart attack in 1958, and remained mostly bedridden till his death.

Forest got married and divorced three times. His fourth marriage was to Marie Mosquini in 1930.

Lee de Forest died on June 30, 1961, at the age of 87. After his death, his works were donated to the Perham Electronic Foundation. They are now on display at the Perham Collection of Early Electronics.

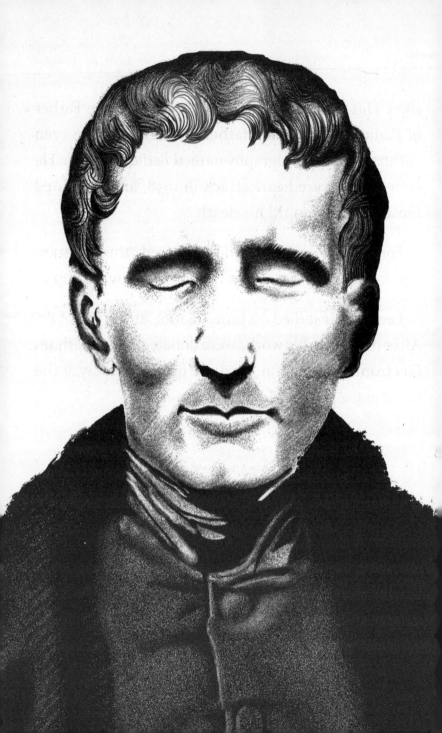

LOUIS BRAILLE

BIRTH : *January 4, 1809*
Coupvray, France

DEATH : *January 6, 1852 (aged 43)*
Paris, France

Louis Braille was a French educator and an inventor, who developed a system of printing and writing, called 'Braille'. It was made to be used by the blind, and this method is still being used today.

Louis Braille was born on January 4, 1809, in Coupvray, France to Simon-René Braille and Monique Braille. His father owned a leather business. He had three siblings. From a very young age, Braille took an interest in his father's shop and used to spend most of his time there. One day, he neglected his father's advice and touched his tools when his father was not in the shop. Louis tried to punch a hole in a piece of leather with an awl, which is a sharp, pointed tool. But the tool slipped from his hand and struck him in the eye. The resultant infection spread to his other eye as well. At the age of five, Louis Braille lost his eyesight entirely. From that point on, he tried to help others like him.

There was no support system for blind people at the time. Most of the time, the blind were forced to become beggars to earn a living. But his parents wanted Braille to continue his studies and have a better future. He went to the local village for his education, where he was taught by the priest. It was difficult for Braille to read or write properly but he still excelled in his studies. The priest at his school suggested that braille be enrolled into a school for the blind for a better future. In 1819, he was sent to attend the only blind school in Paris called the Royal Institute for Blind Youth. He learned to play the cello and the piano there. At school, all the students were taught by the 'Hauy system', a reading system developed by Valentin Hauy. But, the books and the information available to them were limited, and it was hard for students like Braille to learn how to write. The books that were accessible to them were very heavy and took a long time to read.

The inspiration for the Braille system came to Braille in 1821. A French soldier, Charles Barbier, visited his school and introduced a new method that he called 'night writing'. It involved using twelve raised dots, which were connected, to describe different sounds. It was developed to be used by soldiers to pass instructions at night, without the need to talk or use light. Barbier thought he could help blind students with this method, but even soldiers found it difficult to use. The Royal Institute's students tried to use night writing, but for them, too, the method was hard to follow. However, Braille took an interest in Barbier's invention and learned the system on his own. He worked for months to make the system easier. He added mathematical and music codes to it, and finally, he formed a new code. It was easier to read and learn.

Braille went to the director of his school and showed him his new system which could help blind students. In 1829, Braille published the *Method of Writing Words, Music and Plain Song by Means of Dots, for use by the Blind and Arranged for Them.* People loved the effectiveness of the Braille system. The advantage was that blind people could write by using a simple tool with the help of dots. This helped them to learn and gather knowledge. Braille became a teacher at his school and taught geometry, algebra and history. The students loved him as a teacher. He also created a code for musical notes. Children learned how to read and write music with the help of codes.

Another invention by Braille was the 'Deca-point' or 'Raphigraphy', which was a language writing system for the blind that could also be read by the sighted. He tried inventing the typewriting machine that wrote Raphigraphy. Braille didn't live to see the worldwide popularity of his system, and his great contribution to society. He suffered from poor health most of his life. He had tuberculosis.

At the time, effective medicines were not available to treat the disease. He died in 1852, at the age of 43.

After his death, the popularity of the Braille system appealed to the French government. The government made Braille's dot alphabet the official method for blind people to read and write. It was officially called Braille, named after its inventor. By 1990, with the help of the United Nations, the Braille system was adapted to every known language. In 1952, Louis Braille's grave was moved to Paris and he was buried in the Pantheon, where eminent French achievers are buried.

MARIE CURIE

BIRTH: *November 7, 1867*
Warsaw, Poland

DEATH: *July 4, 1934 (aged 66)*
near Sallanches, France

Marie Curie was a Polish-born French physicist. She won the Nobel Prize in Physics and another in Chemistry. She was the first woman ever to win a Nobel Prize in any field. Curie was famous for her work in the field of radioactivity.

Marie Curie's birth name was Maria Sklodowska. She was born on November 7, 1867, in Warsaw, Poland to Bronislawa and Wladyslaw Sklodowski. Both her parents were teachers. Because of her father, Marie developed an interest in mathematics and physics. She was a bright student and had learned to read and write at a very early age. For her education, she went to J. Sikorska and graduated in 1883 with a gold medal.

Marie decided to continue her studies. But in the 1800s, it was uncommon for young women in Poland to attend a university. So, she attended the underground educational establishment known as 'Flying University'. Marie paid for her sister's college tuition, while putting her own dreams on hold. In her free time, she educated herself by reading books. She used to do practical training at the chemical laboratory.

In 1891, she finally attended the Sorbonne University. During this time, she came to be identified as Marie. In 1893, she received her master's degree in physics. And the next year, in mathematics. She soon began her scientific career and studied the different types of steel and their magnetic qualities.

Later, she returned to Paris and pursued her PhD degree. Marie then met scientists Wilhelm Roentgen and Henri Becquerel with whom she worked for many years. She was interested in the rays that were discovered by these scientists. Roentgen had found X-rays and Becquerel had discovered uranium salts. Marie began to conduct experiments and work a little further on these discoveries.

She used two uranium minerals called pitchblende and torbernite. Around 1898, Ma-rie started to work with Pierre Curie. They researched to discover additional substances that emitted radiation. But one day, Marie saw something unusual in the pitchblende material. She had assumed there would be few rays emitted from the uranium in the pitchblende. Instead, Marie noticed a lot of rays. She realized that there was a new, undiscovered element within pitchblende.

Marie was amazed at this discovery. She spent endless hours in the science lab with Pierre Curie to investigate pitchblende and the new element. They ultimately concluded that there were two new elements in pitchblende. These were two new additions to the periodic table. In 1898, a new element, which was also radioactive, was discovered. Marie named it 'polonium', after her homeland, Poland. The same year, another element was named 'radium' as it emitted strong rays. The term 'radioactivity' was coined by Marie Curie, which described elements that emitted strong rays.

Later, the two scientists were able to retrieve polonium and radium in their pure forms from the mineral pitchblende. In 1902, they finally separated radium salt. For the next few years, Marie published many scientific papers about her work on radioactivity.

In 1903, the Nobel Prize in Physics was awarded to Marie and Pierre Curie, as well as to Becquerel for their work in radiation. Marie was at the height of her career. She received a doctorate from the University of Paris. And in 1911, Marie was awarded the Nobel Prize in Chemistry for the two elements. She became the first person to have won two Nobel Prizes.

Marie also played a significant part during World War I. Marie discovered that X-rays could help doctors determine what was wrong with a wounded soldier.

She even came up with the concept of X-ray machines and trained people to run them. She installed many mobile radiological vehicles and units on the field. After the war, she wrote a book named *Radiology in War.*

Marie married Pierre Curie on July 26, 1895. The couple had two daughters. They worked on major experiments that changed the world of science together. Marie died on July 4, 1934, after she suffered from aplastic anaemia due to continued exposure to radiation.

Today, lots of safety measures are followed by scientists to avoid getting overexposed to the rays. As a tribute to Curie, many buildings, universities, roads and museums were named after her.

NICOLAUS COPERNICUS

BIRTH: February 19, 1473
Toruń, Poland

DEATH: May 24, 1543 (aged 70)
Frauenburg, Poland

Nicolaus Copernicus was a well-known astronomer, mathematician, translator, artist and physicist. He was the first astronomer to form a model of the universe in which the sun was the center of the solar system and the planets were situated around the sun. He came up with the theory of a heliocentric solar system. Copernicus was known as the 'Father of Modern Astronomy'.

Nicolaus Copernicus was born on February 19, 1473, in Poland. He had three siblings. His father was a merchant and his family was counted amongst the wealthy. Nicolaus' father died when he was young and he was brought up by his maternal uncle. For his education, he went to St John's School. After he completed his studies, he attended the University of Kra-kow. He took mathematics and painting as his graduation subjects. But soon he started to take an interest in astronomy. He bought many books and got engaged in the subject. In 1497, he joined the University of Bologna to pursue law.

While there, he met the famous astronomer Domenico Maria Novara. Copernicus took lectures from a well-known Polish astronomer and soon assisted Novara in his research. In 1503, he graduated with a law degree and started to teach astronomy to others. Copernicus studied the works of astronomers like Plato and Cicero. He learned about the movement of the Earth, which later on became the basis of his research. He developed a theory that the Earth and other planets orbited the sun. Copernicus didn't share his findings with anyone for many years.

Copernicus moved to Rome in 1500 where he delivered lectures on mathematics. He met George Rheticus, who helped Nicolaus to publish his works. He worked in the Catholic Church for a short period. In 1514, he released his first work studying the universe called *Commentariolus* (Little Commentary) in his circle. It was a collection of letters. He continued to do his research in isolation, without anyone's help. He made most of his astronomical observations about the sun and the planets way before the telescope was invented.

Around 1530, he came up with one of his most significant works, which is still referred to in astronomy, called *De Revolutionibus*. In his book, he explained that the Earth rotates on its own axis once every day and revolves around the sun once every year. And, he correctly described all the planets' positions in the solar system. He revealed why seasons occurred. He also claimed that the distance from the Earth to the sun was much lesser than the distance from the Earth to the other stars.

Copernicus' astronomical model, a heliocentric planetary system, was also created around the same time. His observations differed from the astronomers who came before him. Everyone thought that the universe was a closed space bound by a spherical envelope beyond which there was nothing. But, Copernicus changed how people viewed the universe.

Copernicus' works were not limited to just astronomy. He was also a physician, scholar, economist, translator, mathematician, artist and diplomat.

Most of Copernicus' works were released later in life. Some parts of his research were distributed amongst astronomers. One of them was a young man who discovered his works. If he hadn't found Copernicus' works, they would never have been published. It was only in 1543 that the full book of his works was released.

When his book went to Pope Paul III, the Church rejected his writings. The printer added a note in the book saying that even though the book's theory was unusual, it helped astronomers with their calculations, and that the subject could only be understood by highly educated people. The Church eventually banned the book in 1616. The Catholic Church wasn't the only one to reject Copernicus' ideas. The religious leader Martin Luther also voiced his displeasure about this solar system model.

Due to his pledge to the Church, Copernicus never got married. He died on May 24, 1543, at the age of seventy, in Poland.

NIKOLA TESLA

BIRTH: 1856
Smiljan, Croatia

DEATH: January 7, 1943
New York, USA

Nikola Tesla was a Serbian-American engineer and physicist and one of the most significant inventors of all time. He became famous for inventing an induction motor that ran on alternating current (AC), which was later used in many devices like radars, X-rays and wireless communications. Tesla also conceived the rotating magnetic field, and had more than 300 patents registered in his lifetime.

Nikola Tesla was born in 1856 in Smiljan, Croatia

to Milutin Tesla and Djuka Mandic. His father was a priest and his mother was an inventor who used to make household appliances. He had four siblings. As a kid, he loved reading science and wanted to pursue a career in the same field. For his education, he went to the town's primary school where he studied German, mathematics and religion. In 1870, he went to Higher Real Gymnasium in Karlovac for his higher education. Later, he attended Austria Polytechnic to study science on a scholarship.

Even though Tesla wanted to study physics and mathematics, he started to take a particular interest in electricity. The concept of an AC motor came to him in 1982, while he took a walk in the park. Before he could forget the idea, he quickly sketched the rotating magnetic field in the sand. He went to Paris that year and joined the Continental Edison Company. There, he fixed Direct Current (DC) power plants. Tesla was also able to successfully build a model of the induction motor. But, nobody in Europe took an interest in his invention. So, Tesla moved to New York and got a job with the genius inventor Thomas Edison.

He worked with others and improved the motors that Edison had invented. But, after he had worked for a year, some disagreement occurred between Tesla and Edison. It was about the Edison DC and the Tesla AC. It spread like wildfire and people called the fight between the two great inventors the 'war of the currents'.

Soon, Tesla left the company. He set up his own company to support his inventions. The company was called Tesla Electric Light and Manufacturing. He received thirty patents for his invention in the field of electricity. George Westinghouse was impressed by Tesla's work and offered him a job. He wanted Tesla to continue working on his invention to produce the alternating current. He even supplied him with a laboratory for his experiments.

In 1891, Tesla created various electrical devices. One of them was the 'Tesla Coil', which was a high voltage transformer for the improvement of light. He also made electronic oscillators, meters and X-rays. People witnessed the 'war of the currents' again in 1891. Edison and Tesla took part in a competition to prove which one was better. It was a competition between energy and power. In 1893, Tesla succeeded in lighting up the entire city of Chicago with hundreds of bulbs, without wires. Finally, Tesla won the competition against the Edison DC system.

Tesla was the inventor who installed the first AC power station of the world at Niagara Falls. He was presented with the Order of Danilo, the highest honor for any civilian, by the Kingdom of Montenegro.

Tesla met J.P. Morgan and convinced him to invest in his experiments. With Morgan's financial support, he built a communication tower to power the world. It was the first ever wireless broadcasting system, famously known as 'Wardenclyffe Tower'.

Tesla was always a pioneer in his field. The Tesla Coil, invented in 1891, was used in radios and televisions. But, most of his research went into the wrong hands.

One such incident was when his notes and research on the radio were stolen by Guglielmo Marconi. In 1909, Marconi received the Nobel Prize for the invention of the radio, which was originally Tesla's work. Tesla even filed a lawsuit to get the rights for his invention, but he lost the case. In 1943, the case was reopened, and in the same year, Tesla got the credit for his invention. He was henceforth known as the 'Father of Radio'.

Tesla received the Elliott Cresson Medal in 1894, the John Scott Medal in 1934 and the Order of the White Eagle in 1936. A unit of magnetic induction was named as 'Tesla' in his honor. Also, the Nikola Tesla Award was established for people who made great contributions to the field of electricity. In 1997, *Life* magazine counted Tesla in the '100 most famous people of the last 1,000 years'.

Tesla passed away on January 7, 1943, in New York City.

PHILO FARNSWORTH

BIRTH: August 19, 1906
Beaver, Utah, USA

DEATH: March 11, 1971 (aged 64)
Salt Lake City, Utah, USA

Philo T. Farnsworth was the American inventor of the first-ever functional electronic tele-vision. He was known as the 'Father of Electronic TV'. He made many contributions to the early development of television and communication.

Philo T. Farnsworth was born on August 19, 1906, in Beaver, Utah to Lewis Edwin Farnsworth and Serena Amanda Bastian. He had four siblings, and his family lived in a log cabin. From a very young age, he loved mechanical and electrical things. He won prize money for a magazine contest in which he invented a magnetized car lock. He won a national competition for developing a tamper-proof lock. He once even built an electrical appliance for his family home. For his education, he attended Rigby High School. He excelled in physics and chemistry. For higher education, he went to Brigham Young High School and graduated in 1924. After the death of his father, Philo did multiple jobs to support his family. The idea for the television came to him while he was still in school.

Philo completed his studies and joined the United States Naval Academy for a short while. He then met George Everson and Leslie Gorrell. They both liked Philo's work and offered him a job in their bulk-mailing business. Philo once again shared his idea of the television. He explained the concept of breaking down an image into parallel lines of light to project the image on a screen for people to see. They loved Philo's television idea and offered to fund his research work. The resulting company was named Everson, Farnsworth & Gorrell, and Philo started to carry out his experiments in his new laboratory.

In 1927, Farnsworth developed the first electronic television transmission. He made a camera tube to send the first picture to a receiver that was kept in another room of the laboratory. And over the years, he made modifications in his techniques. Finally, he carried out the first-ever live human images through his television system. Even though Farnsworth was the first person who displayed the transmission of television signals, he had trouble patenting his work. Till the early 1930s, Farnsworth fought legal battles for his inventions with the inventor Vladimir Zworkyin.

In 1931, Farnsworth moved to Philadelphia and joined the Philco Radio Company. The company helped him financially to continue doing his research in the Philadelphia laboratory. Next year, he met another inventor named John Logie Baird, who worked on his TV system but needed help to make it into an electronic TV system.

Farnsworth left the company to travel to Europe. He kept on doing research work. Everyone noticed his talent and skills. He was soon hired by various technology companies and universities. He did many experiments to study infant incubators, radar, atomic energy, and nuclear power. In 1938, he set up his own company and named it Farnsworth Television and Radio Corporation. He was the director of research at the agency, and started selling electronic televisions to households. Farnsworth eventually got approved by the Radio Corporation of America (RCA). He began to be known as the 'Father of Electrical Television'. He also obtained the patent for the television.

In 1951, Farnsworth Television and Radio Company was acquired by International Tele-phone and Telegraph (ITT). Farnsworth's major works came out during this time. He worked for long hours in his basement lab which was 'the cave' for him. He introduced many concepts like warning signals for defense, radar equipment, submarine detection devices, and an infrared telescope. He created the PPI Projector that was later used as an air traffic control system.

Farnsworth's significant contributions to science and his technology earned him several awards in his career. He was included in the Walt Disney World's Inventor's Circle. In 1999, Farnsworth was mentioned in *Time* magazine's 'The Most Important People of the Century' list.

Farnsworth got married to Elma Gardner on May 27, 1926. The couple had four sons.

He died on March 11, 1971, after he suffered from pneumonia. He was honored with the Eagle Scout Award posthumously. As a tribute, a statue was built for this American inventor in the National Statuary Hall Collection. He was called one of the ten greatest mathematicians of his time by the *Scientific American*. In 1983, Farnsworth's stamp was issued by the United States Postal Service.

ROBERT NOYCE

BIRTH: December 12, 1927
Burlington, Iowa, USA

DEATH: June 3, 1990 (aged 62)
Austin, Texas, USA

Robert Noyce was a great American founder, mentor, engineer and inventor. He was the founder of one of the biggest companies, Intel, and the co-founder of Fairchild Semiconductor. He made the microchip that fueled the personal computer revolution and made the Silicon Valley famous. He was dubbed 'The Mayor of Silicon Valley'.

Robert Norton Noyce was born on 12th December, 1927, in Iowa to Ralph Brewster and Harriet May

Norton. His father was a minister, and his mother was known to be a strong-willed, intelligent woman. Everyone in his house was well-educated. So, Noyce's family paid special attention to his studies. Noyce had a sharp mind and was highly intelligent. He attended Grinnell High School and graduated in 1945. He continued his studies and went to Grinnell College to study mathematics and science. Noyce passed with double majors in physics and mathematics in 1949.

Apart from being an excellent student, he liked handicrafts. At the age of twelve, he built a big aircraft with his brother and tested it from the roof of the Grinnell College. In his free time, he used to work on his scientific plans, build various ship models, a bed, a skate sharpener, a xylophone, etc. He tried to join the Air Force, as he had always been interested in aeroplanes. However, he was not selected to be a fighter pilot because he was color blind. After his rejection by the Air Force, Noyce joined the Massachusetts Institute of Technology for a program in physics. He graduated with a doctorate in 1953.

Noyce started his career officially in 1953. His thesis on the transistor helped him to gain knowledge about the technology. He received offers from big companies like IBM and Bell Labs. Noyce rejected both of these offers and joined the television and radio company, Philco Corporation as a research engineer. He worked there for three years and made transistors. In 1956, Noyce moved to California and met one of the inventors of the transistor, William Shockley. He offered Noyce a position in his company, Shockley Semiconductor Laboratories, who were a group of researchers. Noyce didn't work there for very long. He started his own company, Fairchild Semiconductor, and became the largest shareholder in IBM.

His company was a success. He was involved in making transistors and other silicon devices. Seven of his devices got patented, including the integrated circuit. It was a silicon chip that could hold millions of transistors and resistors, and be utilized as an amplifier, timer, computer memory and more. His design was revolutionary in the semiconductor industry.

In 1968, Noyce launched his company, Intel and left Fairchild Semiconductor. He formed the company with two other people. Noyce served as the president of Intel and took the company to new heights. Today, it is the most significant producer of semiconductor chips in the world. Noyce's invention was named as one of the most important inventions of the twentieth century.

The year 1971 was another excellent year for Noyce and his company. He was the first person to create the single-chip microprocessor. This small chip began to sell in the market. It was a considerable advancement of technology by Noyce. His chips were used in every processor and computer. In 1978, Noyce was selected as the chairman of the Semiconductor Industry Association.

Noyce was also known as the 'The Mayor of Silicon Valley'. He changed the work culture there. He gave his employees equal opportunities to expand their skills.

He was honored with many awards for his extraordinary contribution to the semiconductor industry. In 1987, he received the prestigious National Medal of Technology. In 1983, he was inducted to the National Inventors Hall of Fame.

Noyce got married to Elizabeth Bottomley in 1953. But, the couple separated after twe-nty years of marriage. He later married Ann Schmeltz Bowers.

Noyce died on June 3, 1990, after he suffer-ed a severe heart attack. After his death, the Noyce Foundation was formed by his family. The foundation helped in children's education, especially in mathematics and science. The science building in his university, Grinnell College, was named after him as a tribute.

RUDOLF DIESEL

BIRTH: March 18, 1858
Paris, France

Date of Disappearance: September 29, 1913 (aged 55)
en route London

Rudolf Diesel was a German inventor and mechanical engineer known for his invention of the Diesel engine.

Rudolf Christian Karl Diesel was born on March 18, 1858, in Paris, France to Theodor Diesel and Elise Strobel. His father was a book-binder, and his mother worked as a leatherworker. In 1870, Rudolf's family moved to London, but young Rudolf had to stay with relatives to continue his education. It was at this time that he started to love mechanics. At the age of fourteen, he informed his parents that his dream was to become an engineer. After he finished his education, he joined the Industrial School of Augsburg. He was a bright student and did exceptionally well in his studies. Later, he went to the University of Engineering (Polytechnic Institute), Munich. He studied the basis of mechanics and thermodynamics under Professor Karl Paul Gottfried.

He got practical experience in engineering while he worked at the Sulzer Brothers Machine Works. After he earned his college degree, he moved to Paris. He planned to set up his refrigeration and ice plant business. He took help of his former professor, Karl Paul Gottfried to start his business. In 1881, he was appointed as the director of the factory in Paris. During 1884, Diesel developed an ammonia engine development plan. He came up with a theory that involved using electromagnetic waves at high rotation per second, which was a feat in the field of science.

The company Linde Engineering was impressed by Diesel's work and offered him a job in their Berlin office in 1890.

Diesel continued to make machines that ran smoothly and efficiently. He studied a famous French physicist's works. He concluded that it was possible to create four times more effective engines compared to the steam engines used at the time. Then onwards, he began to work on this idea and designed an engine which brought a revolution in the industry. He tested the engine and used the cheapest fuel available, powdered coal. The experiment was successful and he patented it in 1892.

Diesel started to work on his momentous invention of the diesel engine in the same year. He got the patent for a new rational heat engine and then another patent for the 'working method and design for combustion engines'. In 1893, Diesel built the world's first diesel engine and received a patent for his design. He also published a report on his new engine called the *Theory and Construction of a Rational Heat Motor*. It was received positively by people who wanted to know more about his latest invention.

Even though his tests were successful, the engine was not commercially available. He made a few improvements in his engine. The major one was that he replaced the fuel, coal powder, with pure mineral oil. Later, he began to use heavy petroleum. In 1898, Diesel's 25-horsepower model was presented at the Munich Exhibition. His diesel engine began to sell to the public and the automobile industry.

The very first diesel engine was built in Mississippi. It took him six years to complete the final model of the engine. His technology is still used today in marine engines, automobiles, electric power generators, factories, trains, and oil-drilling equipment. After his invention of the engine, more substantial and heavy vehicles were able to run efficiently. For his notable contribution to technology, Diesel was inducted to the Automotive Hall of Fame in 1978.

Diesel married Martha Flasche in 1883. The couple had three children.

Diesel's death is considered as one of the biggest mysteries of all time. On September 29, 1913, at the age of 55, he suddenly disappeared. His cabin in the steamer he was traveling on was found to be empty.

SIR ISAAC NEWTON

BIRTH: *January 4, 1643*
Woolsthorpe, England

DEATH: *March 31, 1727 (aged 84)*
London, England

Sir Isaac Newton was an English physicist, mathematician, scientist and a genius who brought about a scientific revolution in the seventeenth century. Newton is one of the most influential scientists who ever lived. One of his most important works was the law of gravity.

Sir Isaac Newton was born on 4th January, 1643, in England to Hannah Ayscough and Isaac Newton. His father passed away three months before Isaac was born. His mother remarried later. Isaac was brought up by his grandmother. The young Isaac attended the King's School, Grantham, for his primary education. He was very good academically and was one of the top students at his school. His family was not well off, so Isaac also worked to support his family. He left his studies and started working as a farmer. His school principal asked his mother to send him back to the school to finish his studies. And so Isaac graduated with the highest score.

In 1661, Newton went to Trinity College, Cambridge. Attending the university was the most important decision he took in his life. He was able to pursue his interest in mathematics, astronomy and physics. At that time, the education system was based on Aristotle's model, who was a great philosopher. But, Newton was more involved in the modern syllabus and used to read other philosophers' works. Newton became a professor of mathematics. He taught advanced maths. He was also a Fellow of the Royal Society, which is an organization of scientists in the United Kingdom.

In 1665, his university was shut down for two years due to the plague. Thus, Newton came back home. He spent his days studying calculus theories and the law of gravitation. He had soon mastered mathematics. He graduated with an arts degree in 1669.

After completing his education, Newton fully focused on his inventions. His major achieve-ments include the study of optics, telescopes, and the law of gravitation. He spent years studying colors and light before he presented his inventions to the society. He researched with the help of a prism. He proved that sunlight was constituted of all the colors of the rainbow. Newton also explained the concept of white light and how it carried all the colors found in nature.

Newton's second achievement was inventing the telescope. He built a 6-inch telescope that helped him to see Jupiter's moons. He wanted to see faraway objects sharp and clear. The curved glass lenses used in the telescope worked like a prism.

His book on optics and his prism experiments was called *Opticks* (1704). Robert Hooke was also a member of the Royal Society at this time. Hooke found some faults in Newton's optics theory. Newton was not able to take the criticism very well. He had a very bad nervous breakdown. The same year, he lost his mother. He decided to take a break that lasted six years. During this break, Newton came up with the law of gravitation.

He combined the falling of the apple on his head with the idea of the moon orbiting the Earth. Later on, his theory even explained the movement of the planets and the sun.

In 1684, Newton completed his calculations on gravity. Edmund Halley, the famous astro-nomer and mathematician, visited Newton. Halley wanted Newton's help to solve a problem he was facing with one of his experiments. He asked Newton to explain to him the path in which a planet moved around the sun. Halley didn't know that Newton had already solved this question. Newton and Haley theorized that it was an oval track called an 'ellipse'.

He also showed Halley his other scientific work and calculations. Halley was impressed by Newton and encouraged him to share these theories with the world. His major success was when he released the book *The Mathematical Principles of Natural Philosophy* in 1687. The book contained the three laws of motion that set the framework for modern physics. It helped scientists in understanding how the universe worked.

In his later years, Newton became more popular for his scientific work. He formed the well-known formula that calculated the value of Pi, a mathematical constant.

In 1703, Newton became the president of the Royal Society after Robert Hooke passed away. In 1705, he was knighted by the Queen of England.

Isaac Newton died on March 31, 1727, in London, England. He was one of the greatest scientists alongside masterminds like Albert Einstein and Galileo.

STEPHEN HAWKING

BIRTH: *January 8, 1942*
Oxford, England

DEATH: *March 14, 2018*
Cambridge, England

Stephen Hawking was an English physicist, cosmologist and one of the greatest theoretical scientists in the world. He was best-known for his work on black holes and his research on the theory of relativity and quantum physics. He is the author of the widely read scientific book, *A Brief History of Time.*

Stephen Hawking was born on 8th January, 1942 in Oxford, England, to Frank and Isobel Hawking. Stephen's parents were educated and had graduated from Oxford University. His mother was one of the first female students to have studied at such a prestigious college. His father worked as a medical researcher. Stephen had three siblings. Stephen's father wanted him to become a doctor, but from a very young age he had an interest in astronomy.

For his education, he attended St. Albans School. He was an average student in school but always had an interest in science. At the age of seventeen, he got a scholarship to study at Oxford University. Hawking had always wanted to study mathematics, but the subject was not available in the university, so he chose physics. He found the course easy to understand. Even his physics teacher at Oxford stated that he was an exceptional student. After he graduated in 1962, Hawking attended the University of Cambridge to study cosmology and astronomy. He completed his PhD in 1965 with breakthrough research.

Hawking started his career in 1968. He was a member of the Institute of Astronomy in Cambridge. Hawking was curious about black holes and how the universe was created. In 1973, he went to Moscow. There, he came up with his theory of black holes. After some intense studying, he had come to the conclusion that they released radiation.

With this theory, he became a Fellow of the Royal Society the same year. Soon, Hawking received back-to-back significant awards like the Eddington Medal, the Pius XI Gold Medal, the Dannie Heineman Prize and the Maxwell Prize. In 1977, he became a professor and taught gravitational physics. In 1979, Hawking was awarded the Albert Einstein Medal. He was also honored with a doctorate by the University of Oxford.

His other major achievements included his mathematical model based on Albert Einstein's general theory of relativity. In 1988, he published a book called *A Brief History of Time* and later *The Universe in a Nutshell* in 2001. Both of his books became bestsellers, and Hawking was counted as one of the most renowned cosmologists. Hawking explained the creation of the universe and the Big Bang theory in his books. The book was translated into thirty languages.

It was not an easy road to success for Hawking. He went through many hardships. Hawking was only 21 when he was diagnosed with Amyotrophic Lateral Sclerosis (ALS). He was a first-year student at Cambridge University at the time. His motor neuron disease worsened. He began to trip, dropped items and his speech became unclear. He went through a series of tests, and doctors gave him only two and a half years to live.

Hawking was young and ambitious, and the disease didn't stop him from pursuing his dreams. He was paralyzed for most of his life but he still completed his PhD and released most of his major works during these years. As years passed, Hawking became less mobile and began to use a wheelchair.

Hawking met Jane Wilde right before he was diagnosed with his illness. They got married in 1965 and had three children. However, the marriage ended and in 1995,

Hawking married Elaine Manson.

Hawking not only wrote outstanding books but also appeared in many TV shows as a cameo character like in *Star Trek: The Next Generation* and *The Big Bang Theory*. In 2014, a movie based on Hawking's life was released called *The Theory of Everything* starring Eddie Redmayne.

In his lifetime, Hawking received many awards. He won the United States Presidential Medal of Freedom, the Wolf Prize and the Russian Fundamental Physics Prize.

Hawking died on March 14, 2018, in Cambri-dge, United Kingdom.

THE WRIGHT BROTHERS

Wilbur Wright

BIRTH: April 16, 1867
Millville, Indiana, USA

DEATH: May 30, 1912
Dayton, Ohio, USA

Orville Wright

BIRTH: August 19, 1871
Dayton, Ohio, USA

DEATH: January 30, 1948
Dayton, Ohio, USA

The Wright brothers, Orville and Wilbur Wright, were two American inventors, engineers and aviators, who are credited with inventing, constructing and flying the first aeroplane. They are known as the 'Fathers of Modern Aviation'. Their technology is still used in modern aircrafts.

Wilbur Wright was born on April 16, 1867, near Millville, Indiana to Milton Wright and Susan Catherine Wright. And four years later, Orville Wright was born on August 19, 1871, in Dayton, Ohio. Their father worked as a minister in many churches. Due to their father's position as a bishop, the family moved around a lot. The brothers had five other siblings. The Wright brothers grew up in a family where education was considered important. Their parents encouraged them to read and enhance their creativity. It was their father who bought them a toy helicopter. The toy was made in France, and it sparked the curiosity in the Wright brothers' minds. They dreamed of building the same model, one day. They developed an interest in aeronautics.

Both the brothers were bright and excelled in their studies. After Wilbur graduated from high school, he planned on attending Yale University for his higher studies. But in 1885, he was involved in an accident which changed his life. He was badly injured during an ice-hockey game. After this incident, he lost motivation to continue studying. He gave up his dream of studying at Yale. He stayed at home and took care of his ill mother and supported his family.

His brother Orville attended Dayton Central High School. Unlike his brother who was more studious, Orville was more interested in extracurricular activities. In 1889, he opened a printing shop and asked his brother to join him. They started a weekly newspaper called *West Side News* and set up a printing press all by themselves. Wilbur was the editor and Orville worked as the publisher.

In 1892, the Wright brothers opened a bicycle shop, which became very successful amongst the local people. They fixed bicycles and designed new models on their own. They also started to research and design plans for their future projects.

They were influenced by the German aviator Otto Lilienthal, who was known as the 'flying man'. Unfortunately, he died in an accident in 1896. Following this tragedy, the Wright brothers decided to create a safe flying design. They built a glider, which was a light aircraft, designed to fly without an engine. It was like a giant kite. The wings of the aircraft were inspired by birds. They used a concept called 'Wing Warping', which provided the same balance and control as birds' wings did.

After they worked on the model for months, they made the first flight in 1903. They went to North Carolina to test their models because of its strong and windy conditions. However, not many people welcomed their invention. In 1908, they moved to Europe to convince people and sell their designs. In just a few months, people took more interest in their aeroplane models. They soon became famous.

Before the brothers returned to the United States in 1909, they acquired considerable wealth. The same year, they made the world's first flight in a demonstration for the United States Army. It was the world's first military aeroplane and was created by the Wright brothers.

They dedicated their entire lives to the avia-tion industry. They improved their technology and built a modern aircraft. The Wright brothers started the Wright Company in 1909. The same year, they received the Congressional Gold Medal, after they returned to the United States from a successful trip to Europe. They were also awarded gold medals by the state of Ohio and the city of Dayton. They received the Legion of Honor in 1909.

Wilbur suffered from typhoid fever and died in 1912 at his family home. His younger brother, Orville, became president of the company. But, he didn't have much interest in the business side of their work and sold the company in 1915. The Wright brothers never married, and spent their lives inventing and contributing to the society. Orville died on January 30, 1948, after he suffered from a heart attack.

THOMAS EDISON

BIRTH: *February 11, 1847*
Milan, Ohio, USA

DEATH: *October 18, 1931 (aged 84)*
New Jersey, USA

Thomas Edison was one of the greatest American inventors and a proficient business-man. He was best-known for having more than a thousand patents for his amazing inventions. His most famous inventions include the phonograph, the motion picture camera, and the electric light bulb. He was called a 'wizard' and a 'genius' for his contribution to the society.

Thomas Alva Edison was born on February 11, 1847, in Milan, Ohio to Samuel and Nancy Edison. He was the youngest of seven children. Thomas was known as 'Al' in his childhood. His father was a political activist and his mother was a teacher. In 1854, his family moved to Michigan where Thomas spent most of his childhood. Thomas went to public school for a short time. He discontinued his studies in just three months. His mother played a big role in his education, as he was home-schooled by her.

Thomas was also an avid reader. Teachers described him as a poor student, but he did well when taught by his mother. As a young and curious mind, he would conduct experiments in the basement of his home. He had an interest in mechanical things and building objects.

He began to work at the age of twelve. His first business attempt was when he started the *Grand Trunk Herald*. It was the first newspaper which was started on a moving train. The paper was a great success among the masses. Edison made a small laboratory in one of the baggage cars. There, he performed his experiments. His newspaper was also printed in the same laboratory. However, his car caught fire when one of his chemical tests went wrong.

During 1862, Edison learned how to use the telegraph. He took an interest in communication and electricity, which he later experimented with in many of his inventions. In 1862, after he received proper training, he started to work as a telegraph operator in a local office.

At the age of fifteen, Edison was known as a 'tramp telegrapher'. He studied and later tested telegraph technology. He used a set of characters (sequences of dots and dashes) called the Morse code in his telegraph experiments. Slowly, he began to invent things. His first invention, which got patented, was the electric vote recorder.

Edison got his big break after he invented the stock ticker called the Universal Stock Printer, at the age of 22. Edison's invention caught the attention of The Gold and Stock Telegraph Company. The company paid him a lot of money for the rights to the invention. He built a small research laboratory in Menlo Park. It was the first building which was built with the intention of inventing. He offered jobs to many people, who were also inventors in his research lab.

The three greatest inventions of his career were the phonograph, the lightbulb and the motion picture camera. The phonograph was his first big invention. The device, invented in 1877, was used to record. People started to call him the 'Wizard of Menlo Park' and the 'Inventor of the Age'.

His second big invention was the practical light bulb in 1879. His electric light system delivered light to the entire city. He had started the Edison Electric Light Company just a year ago. To supply electricity to everyone, he developed safety fuses and on/off switches for light sockets.

He also improved on his previous experiments, particularly the phonograph.He developed the first commercially viable fluoroscope and the first talking doll.

Edison's third major invention was the mot-ion

picture camera. He worked with William Dickson to build the motion picture camera. His practical invention contributed to the development of movies.

Edison was not only an inventor, but also a great businessman. In his later years, he developed the storage battery to power electric cars. The first battery was used by Henry Ford and became a huge success. During World War I, he helped the government by building submarine radars for them.

Edison got married twice. He was the father of six children.

Thomas Edison died on October 18, 1931, due to diabetes. After his death, people paid tribute to this great inventor. Edison's birthday is noted as National Inventor's Day.

TIM
BERNERS-LEE

BIRTH: June 8, 1955
London, England

Tim Berners-Lee is a British computer scientist who has to his credit one of the most revolutionary inventions of the twentieth century, the World Wide Web (WWW).

Timothy Berners-Lee was born on June 8, 1955, in London, England, to Mary Lee Woods and Conway Berners-Lee. He has three siblings. His love for computers came from his computing family. For his education, he attended London's Emanuel School till 1973. After he graduated, he joined the Queen's College at the University of Oxford. In 1976, he received a degree in physics.

Lee got his first job as an engineer at a tele-communications company in Plessey. During the 1970s, he worked with various companies. In 1980, he was hired by CERN as an independent software engineer. He came up with a programme which used hypertext, a language that allows embedding links in text. His programme was called 'Enquire'. The same programme was also used to build the World Wide Web.

In 1981, he worked at John Poole's Image Computer Systems Limited. He worked there for three years and gained lots of technical knowledge. A few years later, he went back to CERN. He noticed that hundreds of employees worked at the organization and it was getting difficult for them to manage and share information with each other. He thought of making an easier and more efficient method for data sharing. He presented his plans to CERN. He explained how he planned on distributing information all over the internet.

Around 1989, he was entirely focused on building

the web. He created three new systems to make the new web work. They were HTML, HTTP and URL. The first one was the Hypertext Markup Language (HTML), a computer language for webpages. The second was the Hypertext Transfer Protocol (HTTP) used for recovering documents. And the last one was the Universal Resource Locators (URLs), which are the web addresses.

In 1990, with CERN, Lee launched the world's first website. The first website was simply called *info.cern. ch*. It was put online in 1991. The site was built to show how people could share information easily and also gather it all in one location.

To improve his web, he founded the W3C (World Wide Web Consortium). He decided to keep the technologies royalty-free and open to the public. This meant that anyone could use them and reap the benefits. It changed people's lives. Lee's WWW's impact was the same as that of the invention of the television or the radio, if not more.

In 1999, Lee became the first holder of the 3Com Founders Chair. Lee even protected the freedom of the web. He made it possible to open the information-sharing platform for everyone. He gave every person the right to use the web and advocated for net neutrality. He did not want the government to get involved or put any restrictions on the usage of the WWW.

Not only is Lee a great innovator, but he is also a great teacher and author. In 2004, he worked as a professor in the computer science department at the University of Southampton. In 2006, he became the co-director of the Web Science Trust. The trust was started to study the World Wide Web and propose solutions for its usage and design. In 2009, he worked as a director of the World Wide Web Foundation. Lee worked with the UK government on a project, which made UK data more accessible to the public. Its website was called *data.gov.uk*. He continued to work with the government and became a member of the Public Sector Transparency Board.

Lee also wrote about the importance of the internet.

In 1999, he published his first book called *Weaving the Web: The Original Design and Ultimate Destiny of the World Wide Web*. It narrates his journey of creating the web and the planning that went into it. In 2006, he released *A Framework for Web Science*, his second book, co-authored by other computer scientists and researchers.

Lee is a recipient of many awards and honors. In 1995, he received The Software System Award. In 1999, he was named as one of the '100 Most Important People of the 20th century' by *Time* magazine. In the year 2004, he was appointed Honorary Knight Commander of the Order of the British Empire and was awarded the Order of Merit for his 'services to the global development of the internet'.

Lee is one of five Internet and web pioneers, who were awarded with the Queen Elizabeth Prize for Engineering. He was even dubbed as 'the man who changed the world'. Lee is an inspiration and sensation for his invention which has shaped our society.

Lee was married and divorced twice. He is the father of two children.

QUESTIONS

Q.1. Who is the 'Father of Modern Physics'?

Q.2. Who discovered penicillin?

Q.3. Which prize did Dmitri Mendeleev win for his complete textbook of organic chemistry?

Q.4. Which inventor is known as the 'Father of Railways'?

Q.5. Which inventor's last name is included as a unit of power in the International System of Units?

Q.6. Who discovered oxygen?

Q.7. Which year was the first book written in Braille released?

Q.8. Who was the first woman to win the Nobel Prize in any field?

Q.9. Which university did Nicolaus Copernicus attend?

Q.10.   Nikola Tesla moved to New York and obtained work with which famous inventor?

Q.11. What was Tim Berners-Lee recognized for?

Q.12. Who is known as the 'Father of Modern Aviation'?

Q.13. What is the full form of ALS?

Q.14. What were the three new systems to make the new World Wide Web work?

Q.15. Which year did the Wright brothers take their first flight?

Q.16. Which books did Stephen Hawking write?

Q.17. Which invention is Rudolf Diesel famous for?

Q.18. What is Robert Noyce's company called?

Q.19. In which year did Philo Farnsworth finally invent his version of the television?

Q.20. Who is the 'Father of Modern Astronomy'?

Q.21. Which two elements did Marie Curie and her husband discover?

Q.22. What was the name of the company that Lee de Forest founded?

Q.23. Who was the founder of Mercedes Benz?

Q.24. What did Louis Braille invent?

Q.25. Who invented the Audion vacuum tube?

Q.26. What did Robert Noyce invent?

Q.27. What were the other inventions of Philo Farnsworth, apart from television?

Q.28. What is the name of the astrono-mical model that Nicolaus Copernicus introduced and what is it about?

Q.29. What is the name of the first book printed with the movable type?

Q.30. What did Johannes Gutenberg invent?

DID YOU KNOW?

1. Albert Einstein had speech problems as a child, and his teacher thought he wasn't very smart.

2. Alexander Graham Bell made the first cross-country telephone call in 1915. He called Thomas Watson.

3. Marie Curie was a professor of physics at the Sorbonne, and she was the first woman to hold this post.

4. Marie Curie and fellow scientist Albert Einstein were good friends.

5. Thomas Edison was partially deaf.

6. *Mary had a Little Lamb* was the first sound recorded on the phonograph, it was recorded by Thomas Edison.

7. Benjamin Franklin didn't patent many of his inventions and allowed people to use them for free.

8. There are around twenty complete copies of the Gutenberg Bible in existence today.

9. As a child, Eli Whitney, built a fiddle in his father's workshop.

10. Stephen Hawking was born on the 300th anniversary of the death of the famous scientist Galileo.

11. The Wright brothers designed the plane after studying how birds used their wings.

12. Rudolf Diesel got several German and American patents for his engine design.

13. Stephen Hawking has co-written many children's books with his daughter Lucy.

14. Braille learned to play both the cello and the organ in a small orchestra at his school.

16. Orville Wright's birthday, which is on August 19th, is also National Aviation Day.